Lazy Days of Summer

By Judy Young and Illustrated by Kathy O'Malley

Sleeping Bear Press™

310 North Main Street, Suite 300
Chelsea, MI 48118
www.sleepingbearpress.com

© 2007 Thomson Gale, a part of the Thomson Corporation.
Thomson, Star Logo and Sleeping Bear Press are trademarks
and Gale is a registered trademark used herein under license.

Printed and bound in China.

First Edition

10 9 8 7 6 5 4 3 2 1

Library of Congress Cataloging-in-Publication Data

Young, Judy.
Lazy days of summer / written by Judy Young ; illustrated by Kathy O'Malley.
p. cm.
Summary: "Using poetry and prose, this book relives many of the familiar
games of childhood and invites young readers to join along in playing Kick the
Can, Monkey in the Middle, and Double Dutch jump rope. Origins of the games
are also included"—Provided by publisher.
ISBN-10: 1-58536-241-7
ISBN-13: 978-1-58536-241-7
1. Games—Juvenile literature. I. O'Malley, Kathy, ill. II. Title.

GV1203.Y67 2007
790.1'922—dc22
                    2006026101

To my first playmates,
my sisters Robbie, Lindy, and Kristie,
And all of our children
Jill, Christa, Brett, Reid, Deanna, Adrianna, and Ryan.
J.Y.

To everyone who ever played Tag with me,
if you're reading this — You're It!
K.O.

Playing games seems to be a natural characteristic  of being human. The earliest artifacts of man show pictures of games being played. Many games have been passed along for thousands of years. Some have remained almost the same while others have developed into many variations. Although different cultures have played games in different ways, the same types of games are played worldwide. No matter if your

 variation of a game is the same or different from the ones in this book, games are fun to play. So, go outside, play by yourself, find a friend, or a whole neighborhood of friends. But whomever you play with and whatever you play, have fun!

On lazy days of summer, I go out to play

Jumping Rope is a game that I play everyday.

With all of my neighbors, my family, and friends,

We have lots of fun until the day ends.

The rope starts to turn and I jump with my feet

As I sing out a song with the same rhythmic beat,

Turn around, touch the ground, first jump slowly, then fast.

How many more jumps do you think I will last?

⋆ Did You Know? ⋆

★ From ancient Egyptian times and up through the 1800s in America, jumping rope was thought of as a boy's activity. It was considered too strenuous and was often forbidden for girls. Today we know that jumping rope is fun and great exercise for both boys and girls.

★ You can jump rope by yourself or two friends can turn a rope while a third friend jumps. Learn to "run in the front door" as the rope turns toward you, or "run in the back door" as it turns away from you. For a challenge, jump "Double Dutch" with two ropes turning at the same time in opposite directions!

★ Reciting a rhyme while jumping helps keep your rhythm. Some jump rope rhymes give directions to the jumpers or turners, such as "turn around and touch the ground," "red hot" (turn fast), or "high water" (turn the rope about a foot off the ground). Some rhymes count your jumps, such as "Popcorn popping, pop, pop, pop, how many times can I hop, hop, hop? One, two, three, four..." Others invite someone to jump with you: "Jordan, quick as you can be, run in here and jump with me." Make up your own jump rope rhyme!

On lazy days of summer, I go out to play

Hopscotch is a game I play everyday.

With all of my neighbors, my family, and friends,

We have lots of fun until the day ends.

On one foot, then two feet, then two feet, then one,

In squares my feet land 'til the pattern is done.

Like a toad hopping quickly to get where he goes,

I hop without touching a line with my toes.

★ Did You Know? ★

★ For hundreds of years, children have hopped their way across hundreds of hopscotch patterns. Even Roman soldiers played hopscotch! Carrying another soldier on their back, they played games of speed on hopscotch courts up to 100 feet long.

★ Hopscotch did not get its name from Scotland. "Scotch" meant "scratch" and referred to the pattern scratched in the dirt. Some patterns are made of squares, some look like wheels, and some are snail-shaped spirals.

★ To play, draw a hopscotch pattern, numbering the spaces. Toss a marker, such as a rock, into square one. You hop over squares with markers, so hop into square two, then square three. Keep going, hopping on one foot. If squares are side by side, land on two feet, one in each square. At the end, hop up, turn around, and land in the same place. Continue hopping back down the pattern. When you get to the marker, pick it up and hop on out of the pattern. On the next round, throw your marker in square two, then square three and so on. Your turn is over if your marker lands in the wrong square, you touch a line when hopping, or you lose your balance.

On lazy days of summer, I go out to play

Tag is a game I play everyday.
With all of my neighbors, my family, and friends,
We have lots of fun until the day ends.

IT might be a monster, IT might be a bear,
IT might be a dragon just trying to scare.
But whatever IT is, I'll run quickly away.
I won't let IT tag me this hot summer day.

Safe

⋆ Did You Know? ⋆

★ "Not IT, not IT, not IT!" is heard across the neighborhood until one person is left, with a chorus of voices claiming "You're IT!" IT chases everyone around until he tags someone and screams, "Tag, you're IT!"

★ There are many versions of the simple tag game. In Ball Tag, IT throws a ball to tag a runner. When you are tagged in Freeze Tag, you "freeze" like a statue until another runner touches you to unfreeze you. If someone is frozen three times, he becomes IT. Some tag games have a safety zone, such as on a porch or a tree, where runners are safe from being tagged. In Hang Tag, climb a tree or hang from monkey bars. You are safe if you are not touching the ground. At night, play Flashlight Tag. IT has a flashlight and you are tagged if the light shines on you!

★ In "What Time Is It, Mr. Wolf?" players follow "Mr. Wolf" around asking him what time it is. The wolf may give any answer, such as "3 o'clock," or "bedtime." However, when he answers "time for dinner," he turns and chases players back to a safety zone. Whoever he tags becomes Mr. Wolf.

On lazy days of summer, I go out to play

Jacks is a game I play everyday.
With all of my neighbors, my family, and friends,
We have lots of fun until the day ends.

I scatter a handful of stars on the ground
And toss up a ball, like a moon it is round.
Then I scoop up the stars and I capture the moon,
I have fun playing jacks. I play all afternoon.

Did You Know?

★ Knucklebones and chuckstones! These are other names for the game of jacks! The ancient Greeks and Romans played with sheep knucklebones. They tossed up one knucklebone, scooped up some more, and then caught the tossed one before it hit the ground. Other ancient cultures played chuckstones (chuck means toss) with stones, seeds, shells, wooden cubes, or small bags of rice.

★ Today, when we play jacks we toss up a small ball, pick up star-shaped metal pieces and catch the ball after it bounces once. In the first round, called "onesies," one jack is scooped up at a time. In "twosies," two jacks are scooped up. If the ball bounces twice, the wrong number of jacks is picked up, or other jacks are touched, that player's turn is over. Rounds continue and the first to complete "tensies" wins.

★ **Try these challenge rounds!**
Eggs in a Basket: Jacks are picked up and placed in the other hand before the ball is caught.
No Bounce: Like in the ancient knuckle-bone games, the ball is caught before it touches the ground.
In the Cave: The nontossing hand is cupped with its side on the ground, forming a "cave." Jacks are slid into the "cave" instead of being picked up.

On lazy days of summer, I go out to play

Fishing *is something I do everyday.*
With all of my neighbors, my family, and friends,
We have lots of fun until the day ends.

Live bait

With swivels and spinners, sinkers and spoons,
And a bobber that floats like a red and white moon,
I cast out my line and patiently wait
'Til a fish swims along and grabs hold of my bait.

✦ Did You Know? ✦

★ For thousands of years people have been fishing: some with traps, some with nets, and some with rods and reels. There are hundreds of types of fish and hundreds of ways to catch them, but whether you visit a stream or a river, a pond or a lake, a summer day of fishing can be packed with fun and discovery.

★ Bait your hook and cast your line. As you are waiting for a bite, relax, look around and discover the uniqueness of nature near the water. You may see a crawdad scoot backward to hide under a rock. A dragonfly may hover close by, or a newt may be found hiding in wet leaves. You may hear frogs croak or see a fish leap out of the water. Do you see a great blue heron standing perfectly still in the shadows? He's fishing, too! Suddenly, you'll feel a tug on your line. You've got a bite! Quickly, snap the rod back to set the hook and slowly reel in your catch. Whether you catch and release or take your fish home for dinner, you can't beat the excitement of pulling in a fish!

★ Remember, be safe around water, and follow your state's fishing laws.

On lazy days of summer, I go out to play

Kick the Can is a game I play everyday.
With all of my neighbors, my family, and friends,
We have lots of fun until the day ends.

The can clanks and clatters, it rolls down the street.
I run to my hideout on quick-moving feet.
You'll never find me, I'm "Invisible Man,"
But now here you come! I'll run quick, kick the can!

✦ Did You Know? ✦

★ Hide and seek games are very old and were developed in imitation of stalking and hunting wild animals. However, you will scare all the wild animals away if you play Kick the Can, the noisiest version of Hide and Seek!

★ To play, place a can in the middle of a "home base" area. One player, IT, closes her eyes and counts to 50 while others run and hide. Then IT looks for the hiders. When IT sees a hider, she calls out "One, two, three, I see _____," telling who and where the hider is. They both race back to the can. If the hider kicks the can first, the hider hides again. If IT protects the can first, by putting her foot on it, the hider becomes a prisoner at home base.

★ While IT looks for other hiders, another player can rescue prisoners by sneaking up, kicking the can and yelling "All free!" However, if IT sees a rescuer coming and protects the can first, the rescuer becomes a prisoner, too. The game continues until all players are captured.

On lazy days of summer, I go out to play

Monkey in the Middle I play everyday.

With all of my neighbors, my family, and friends,
We have lots of fun until the day ends.

I leap up and down, jumping this way and that.
I even try grabbing that ball with my hat.
Like a caged monkey, in the middle I'm stuck
But I'll soon catch that ball if I have any luck.

★ Did You Know? ★

★ Do you feel like a monkey, jumping all around? You will if you play Monkey in the Middle. This game is also called Keep Away.

★ There are several versions of the game. In one version there are two "tossers." There may be any number of "monkeys in the middle," standing between the tossers. A tosser tosses a large rubber ball to another tosser, trying to keep a monkey from catching it. If a monkey catches the ball, the person who tossed it becomes a monkey and the one that caught it gets to toss. Therefore, there are only two tossers at a time.

★ In another version, instead of replacing a tosser when a monkey catches the ball, the monkey that catches the ball becomes an additional tosser. The game starts with two tossers and the number of tossers increases as the game continues until there is just one "monkey in the middle."

★ The opposite of this game is Dodge Ball. In Dodge Ball, instead of trying to keep the ball away from players in the middle, the tossers try to hit a player with the ball. If a player is hit, he and the tosser change places.

On lazy days of summer, I go out to play

Sharks and Minnows is a game I play everyday.
With all of my neighbors, my family, and friends,
We have lots of fun until the day ends.

Minnows and dolphins and swordfish and whales
Swim through the pool with their fins and their tails,
Until a shark comes with his teeth and his bite,
Then, they scatter and scoot and swim off in a fright.

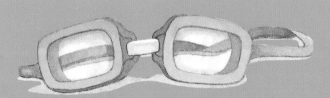

⋆ Did You Know? ⋆

★ If you get the chance to go to a city pool, or maybe you have one in your neighborhood or backyard, it is fun to pretend to be different sea creatures. Keep your arms to your sides and kick both feet together to be a dolphin or a mermaid. Push off the bottom of the pool, jumping up into the air and splashing down on your side like a whale. Sit on the bottom and blow bubbles like a clam. Or gather up your friends and become Sharks and Minnows!

★ Choose someone to be a shark. The shark stands in the middle of the pool. All the other players are minnows. They stand on one side of the pool. When the shark yells, "Swim, minnows, swim!" the minnows must swim to the other side of the pool without the shark tagging them. However, the shark has to keep one hand on his hip, forming a triangle like a shark's fin, swimming and tagging minnows with only one hand. A minnow who gets tagged also becomes a shark until all minnows are caught.

On lazy days of summer, I go out to play

Marbles is a game I play everyday.
With all of my neighbors, my family, and friends,
We have lots of fun until the day ends.

A midnight blue shooter I have in my bag
And right through its center is a golden zigzag
That looks, when I shoot it, like lightning is flashing
Toward a rainbow of marbles when my thumb sends it crashing.

★ Did You Know? ★

★ Are you a mibster? You are if you play marbles! You "knuckledown," shooting your "taw" at marbles called aggies, cat's eyes, clearies, bumboozers, and peewees. If you play for keepsies, you get to keep the "kimmies" you hit out of the ring. If you play "for fair," everyone gets his marbles back.

★ Marbles have been played for over 3,000 years and there are many versions of the game. One of the most common is Ring Taw. To play, draw a ring about two to three feet wide on a flat surface. Put all the "kimmies" (target marbles) in the middle. Keeping your knuckles touching the ground outside the ring line, hold your shooter marble, or "taw," with your index and middle fingers. Curl your thumb behind the taw and flip it out, aiming at the kimmies. If your taw knocks a kimmie out of the ring, keep it and shoot again, shooting from wherever your taw stopped. If your taw goes outside the ring, or you don't knock out a kimmie, your turn is up. Play until all kimmies are hit out of the ring. Whoever has the most is the winner.

On lazy days of summer, I go out to play

Kickball is a game I play everyday.
With all of my neighbors, my family, and friends,
We have lots of fun until the day ends.

A red rolling ball like a rolling red sun
Comes moving toward me and I kick and I run.
Now it's coming again, oh, how quickly we race!
Will the ball or will I be the first to reach base?

⋆ Did You Know? ⋆

"You're Up!" But not to bat, to kick!

★ Invented in the mid-1900s in the United States, kickball quickly became a favorite playground game. It is played a lot like baseball except instead of hitting a ball with a bat, a large rubber ball is rolled to home plate and kicked. The kicker then runs bases, just like in baseball, making a point when he comes in to home plate.

★ There are four ways to get a runner out: catch the kicked ball before it touches ground; throw the ball to the first baseman before the runner gets there; tag the runner with the ball; or throw the ball at the runner and hit him below the shoulders. (If the ball hits him in the head, he's not out.) After three outs, the other team is up to kick.

★ If you don't have a lot of players, use "ghost runners." When all teammates are on base, the first kicker announces, "Ghost runner." He then goes back to kick. The ghost "runs" as many bases as the kicker does for that kick. A ghost can even score a point!

★ Play for a certain number of innings, or until your mom calls you in for supper!

On lazy days of summer, I go out to play

Relays and races I run everyday.

With all of my neighbors, my family, and friends,

We have lots of fun until the day ends.

We try to go fast but together we're tied,

We're a three-legged monster who's trying to stride

'Cross the grass toward the finish line, but, again, here we fall!

Do you think it'd be faster if together we'd crawl?

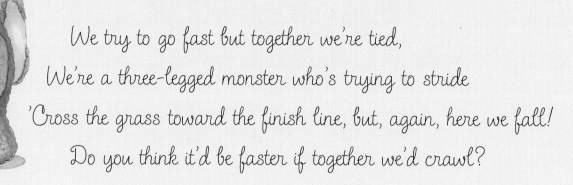

⋆ Did You Know? ⋆

★ The first Olympic Games, in 776 B.C., held just one event, a fast foot race called a sprint. Since then, hundreds of kinds of races have been run.

★ Although speed is the main goal of races, it is fun to add challenges. In a Duck Ball race, a ball is held between the racer's knees, making him wobble like a duck. You may race rolling a peanut with your nose, carrying an egg on a spoon, or balancing a book on your head. Racers hold a partner's feet while she walks on her hands in a wheelbarrow race. A crab race has racers walking on hands and feet, their backs toward the ground. In a caterpillar race, teams sit in a line. Each racer holds the ankles of the teammate in back of them. They look like caterpillars inching along. A racer in a newspaper race has two sections of a newspaper. Standing on one, he places the other in front of him and steps on it. Then, he picks up the first section and puts it in front to step on. He continues in this manner until he reaches the finish line.

★ Be creative! Make up your own race. May the fastest one win!

On lazy days of summer, I go out to play

Jewelry from flowers I make everyday.
With all of my neighbors, my family, and friends,
We have lots of fun until the day ends.

I look for some flowers my mother calls weeds,
Blooming from nearly invisible seeds.
I turn them to necklaces, bracelets, and crowns.
I'm the prettiest princess in all of the town.

✯✯ Did You Know? ✯✯

★ It is fun to spend summer days exploring nature. Lie in the grass looking at big puffy clouds and imagine what they look like. Elephants? A fish followed by a dinosaur? Watch a honeybee at a flower. How many flowers does he visit before he flies away? Swing in a hammock, looking for birds. Do you hear different songs? Can you find which bird is singing which song? After a summer rain, jump in puddles, look in the sky for rainbows, or in the garden for earthworms. Or make your own rain to run through with a sprinkler! At night, catch fireflies and look for shooting stars.

★ Become the king or queen of your backyard with flower jewelry. To do this, pick some flowers, such as clover or dandelions, making sure you get the stem. Make a chain by tying a stem of one flower around the stem of another right underneath the flower head. Wear your chain as a necklace or a crown and pretend to fight dragons, save princesses or search for treasures. You may find a beautiful rock, a gorgeous butterfly, or an interesting insect.

A Note To Parents:

Today, in the age of television and computers, physical games have taken on a new importance. In recent years there have been growing concerns regarding the sedentary lifestyles of our children, resulting in childhood obesity and health problems. There have also been concerns about the increase of learning difficulties and decrease in social interaction skills. Encouraging children to get outside and play games is an answer to these concerns. Playing physical games has obvious benefits to children's physical health and well-being. In addition, games enhance gross and fine motor development and eye/hand coordination. Games also help to stimulate academic success, allowing children to meaningfully discover concepts through the power of observation and deductive reasoning. In some games, children are directly practicing academic skills, such as division when playing jacks. Through games, children also learn to handle life's social challenges. The importance of loyalty, cooperation, and following directions, as well as how to interact verbally, take leadership roles, and handle competition and confrontation, are not readily learned with even the best educational computer games.

So turn off the television, shut down the computer, and send your child out to play a game. Better yet, go out and play with your child and their friends.

Judy Young

Judy Young loves to play! Games are a daily activity at her home in the country near Springfield, Missouri. At lunch she plays cribbage with her husband, Ross, and on hot summer evenings she plays horseshoes and croquet with her daughter and son. Even her dogs like to play catch! However, Judy's favorite things to play with are words! Arranging ideas into a wide variety of poetic styles is like playing with a puzzle where words are the pieces. "What's fun," she says, "is that you never know exactly what the poem puzzle is going to look like, until it is done!"

Judy shares her knowledge and love of poetry by visiting elementary, middle school, and high school classes. She has taught poetry writing classes at Drury University's precollege programs and conducts poetry writing workshops for both students and educators. Judy is Youth Work Director for Missouri State Poetry Society, and the editor of the Society's anthology, *Grist*. Judy is the author of two other Sleeping Bear Press books, *S is for Show Me: A Missouri Alphabet* and *R is for Rhyme: A Poetry Alphabet*. You can read more about Judy at www.judyyoungpoetry.com

Kathy O'Malley

Kathy O'Malley knew she wanted to be an artist from the age of six. Kathy graduated from Chicago's Columbia College, and has illustrated 41 children's books. Her work can also be found on greeting cards, gift bags, limited-edition collectibles, and decorative home products. This is her second picture book with Sleeping Bear Press. She works from her home studio overlooking her perennial gardens, watched by her two loyal art critics, her spoiled standard poodles. See more of Kathy's illustrations at: www.kathyomalley.com.